Acc. 3983

ANDREW MARVELL
SCHOOL LIBRARY
PLEASE RETURN

dealing with
BULLYING

Yvette Solomon

John Coleman

Wayland

Bullying
Eating Disorders
Relationships
Substance Abuse
Death
Family Break-up

Editor: Deb Elliott

Concept design: Joyce Chester

Book design: Helen White

First published in 1994 by Wayland (Publishers) Ltd
61 Western Road, Hove,
East Sussex BN3 1JD

© Copyright 1994 Wayland (Publishers) Ltd

British Library Cataloguing in Publication Data
Solomon, Yvette
 Bullying - (Dealing With Series)
 I. Title II. Coleman, John III. Series
 371.58

ISBN 0 7502 1227 6

Typeset by White Design
Printed and bound by Canale in Italy

All the people who appear in the photographs in this book are models.

Contents

Only teasing **4**

Helping yourself **11**

Getting adults involved **20**

What makes a bully? **28**

The importance of friends **34**

Group work notes **40**

Helping agencies and organizations **42**

Resources **44**

Glossary **46**

Index **48**

Only teasing

Nobody can be sure exactly how much bullying goes on in schools. What we do know is that bullies exist in all kinds of schools, from nurseries through to secondary. When a group of thirteen- to sixteen-year-olds was asked how often they were bullied, one in every five said they were bullied sometimes, and one in every ten admitted that they bullied other people sometimes. This means that quite a few people get involved in some way.

Being bullied can be a living nightmare. Victims, often people without much self-confidence and few close friends in the first place, are likely to lose all belief in themselves and become even more isolated. It is also a fact that a number of young people have died, either as a direct result of bullying or because they've been driven to suicide when they could no longer stand it.

Bullying carries on because of the fear it creates, not just for the victim, but for friends and others who witness the bullying going on. In the end, it becomes a vicious circle of fear and threats. In order to stop bullying, it is necessary to break that circle once and for all.

What do we mean by bullying?

Sue complained that she was being bullied by her friends. They called her 'slut' and 'cheap' because she had highlights in her hair and because they said she dressed up too much. But were Sue's friends really bullying her, or were they only teasing? Where and how do you draw the line between the two?

Some people would say that teasing is good-natured fun that all friends join in with from time to time. They think that someone who doesn't like being teased is just a wimp who can't take a joke. But bullying is very different to teasing; so how do you tell the difference?

If it stops being fun, if the teasing becomes nasty and one-sided and is really meant to hurt, it becomes bullying.

▶ Teasing isn't really meant to be taken seriously. It's light-hearted and jokey and isn't intended to hurt anyone. It's often a two-way process: when someone's being teased they'll usually give as good as they get.

◀ Victims of bullying can feel lonely, isolated and deeply unhappy. What can they do? Is there any way out of their living nightmare?

ONLY TEASING

Different kinds of bullying and the problems they can cause

There are many different ways of being horrible to someone, and some are more obvious than others.

Calling someone names, shouting at them or making threats or spreading nasty rumours about them are all forms of verbal bullying. Despite what some people think, name-calling does hurt. Someone who's being bullied in this way can end up dreading going to school every day, and losing all his or her self-confidence.

Hitting and kicking someone, beating them up or threatening to unless they hand over money or possessions is physical bullying. Apart from the pain involved in any particular incident, victims of this sort of bullying often carry the hurt with them into later life. Adults who've been bullied physically as children often find it hard to build trusting relationships with others. They have trouble believing that anyone could like them.

▶ **Gang bullying is when a group of people picks on one person. This is the worst and most cowardly form of bullying. It is also distressing for the victim, who is made to feel even more isolated.**

BULLYING

ONLY TEASING

Another kind of bullying involves a group of people getting together and ganging up on an individual in some way. For example, the group might suddenly decide to stop talking to the person they've singled out. Or they might not let him or her join in with anything they're doing. People who get involved in this sort of group bullying may not want to, but feel that unless they do they'll not be allowed to be part of the gang any more. This would be hurtful and isolating for anyone. But for teenagers, the threat of being excluded from a group is particularly threatening.

▼ **Friends can sometimes have a bad effect. If your friends are putting pressure on you, or causing you too much hassle, think carefully about the sort of person you want to be.**

Another way group bullying, or peer pressure, works is to force people into doing things they wouldn't do otherwise, such as joy-riding or shop-lifting. Anyone who refuses to join in is made to feel small and pushed out of the gang.

Racial or sexual harassment are types of bullying too. Racial harassment can include racist remarks. One of the many callers

BULLYING

to the Childline organization, set up so that any child with a problem at home or at school can ring in and talk about it completely confidentially, said that because her mum was French and her dad was Sri Lankan, she was called 'stupid Paki' at school. Not only did the caller have to put up with racist remarks, one day she even had her skirt and blouse torn off, so she was the victim of physical aggression too.

Sexual harassment can involve boys and sometimes male teachers expressing sexist

▲ **All families have their share of quarrels, arguments and divisions. However, sometimes things can go too far, and one family member can feel picked on or even bullied.**

attitudes towards girls, and it can also involve physical abuse.

As we've seen so far, bullying can take many different forms and can involve one person being nasty to another, or whole groups of people ganging up against one or two individuals. But there's

another kind of bullying, and it can be one that's even harder to deal with than the others.

Some children are bullied at home by older brothers and sisters and even parents. They may not realise what's going on because it might have been happening since they were very young and therefore it seems like normal life to them. The person who's doing the bullying may not realise that this is in fact what he or she is doing. He or she might shrug it off as just teasing, or believe that it's the way everyone else behaves.

ONLY TEASING 9

Bullying within families can be verbal or physical in the same way as we saw before. In some cases it can take the form of sexual abuse. Either way, the child or children involved can be made to feel that somehow it's their fault and that there's not much they can do about it.

Like all forms of bullying, this kind relies on the person being bullied keeping quiet about what's happening to him or her. But if you are a victim of any kind of bullying you don't have to suffer in silence. There are lots of different ways of dealing with the problem, even if it involves members of your family, as we shall see in the next chapter.

▶ **Bullying can occur at home as well as at school. If it comes from family members, bullying can be even more difficult to deal with.**

Helping yourself

Feeling good

Bullies often pick their victims because there's something slightly different about them: they might decide to hassle someone because they are small, or wear glasses, or have an unusual accent. But these probably aren't the only reasons a person is singled out for bullying. Some victims *feel* small, *feel* different or *feel* insecure. Basically, they don't feel very good about themselves.

If you are a victim of any kind of bullying, one of the most important ways of dealing with it is to learn how to feel good about yourself. For example, instead of feeling small or left out because you don't have the right clothes or aren't good at the same sports or listen to the same music as other people around you, remember that we're all different. And if someone doesn't like you because you're different, that's their problem, not yours.

▶ **There *are* ways of dealing with bullying. If you are being bullied, think carefully about how you could change your behaviour. The more confident you are the less likely you are to be bullied.**

HELPING YOURSELF **11**

▲ **Whether you are facing physical or verbal bullying, one of the most important ways for you to help yourself is to learn to feel positive about who you are.**

Bullies are often anxious characters who rely on bullying weaker people in order to boost their confidence. So if you can feel and look confident they'll be less likely to pick on you. And when you're under fire, try thinking about all your good qualities - being thoughtful, kind, fun to be with - even if the bullies try to tell you different.

Another way of helping yourself is to learn to recognize your feelings, which is not always easy. It's sometimes hard to own up to feeling left out at school or that a friend has let you down.

But if you can learn to take responsibility for your feelings and that you have a choice about how you feel, even when things go wrong, you can start making positive decisions.

For instance, if a friend doesn't turn up one day you could choose to think it's because they don't like you any more and don't want to see you. On the other hand, you could decide that something must have held them up and that they'll explain when you next see them. The first way is negative and makes you feel as if it's your fault. The second way is more positive and doesn't leave you feeling bad about yourself.

Fight or flight: physical bullying

Being punched or kicked or drawn into any kind of fight can be a frightening experience, especially if you're not a physically confident person. Bullies, on the other hand, will have had plenty of practice at fighting. There might even be a whole gang of them, whereas you're more likely to be on your own. Whatever the situation, the chances are that you'll come off worst if you get involved.

A lot of bullies will try to pick a fight by laying the blame on you. They might accuse you of staring at them or something like that. If so, don't do anything that they can use as an excuse to start a fight, because that's what they want. The best thing you can do is just walk away.

This is easier said than done. The bully, or even your friends, might accuse you of not sticking up for yourself. One way of dealing with this is to simply agree with them, saying that you don't think fighting is a good way of sorting out differences. Another is to refuse to rise to the bait. If you don't react to threats and insults by becoming frightened or angry, if you just stay cool, you'll come over as more confident and the bully might give up.

▼ **How can you change the way you feel about yourself and be more self-confident?**

One good way is to learn to recognize what your feelings actually are. Try to be open and honest, and to take responsibility for *your* feelings and *your* behaviour.

▲ **If you feel you want to fight back, if you are fed up with being considered 'weak', then why not join a self-defence class? This will boost your confidence. Remember, bullies pick on people who are vulnerable, precisely because they are not very confident.**

You could try talking your way out of a situation. Stand up to the bully by pointing out that just because he or she doesn't like you, it doesn't have to end in a fight. Or you could say that you've had enough and that you're going to tell someone in authority what's going on. If possible, try joking your way out by responding to insults with something witty. As before, if you don't look upset or scared, you've got a better chance of getting away.

On the other hand, you might decide that it's better to fight back. In which case, going to self-defence classes might be a good idea. The idea behind these classes is not to turn you into an ace fighter, but to teach you how to protect yourself and how to get out of tricky situations without using violence. And if you learn how to protect yourself, you'll be less frightened of physical violence and aggression. Your confidence will increase, which will decrease your chances of being bullied.

▶ **If you are being picked on by a gang of bullies, remember how groups work. The chances are that quite a few people in the group would not go along with the bullying if they felt they had the choice. They certainly would not be doing it at all if they were on their own.**

14 BULLYING

HELPING YOURSELF

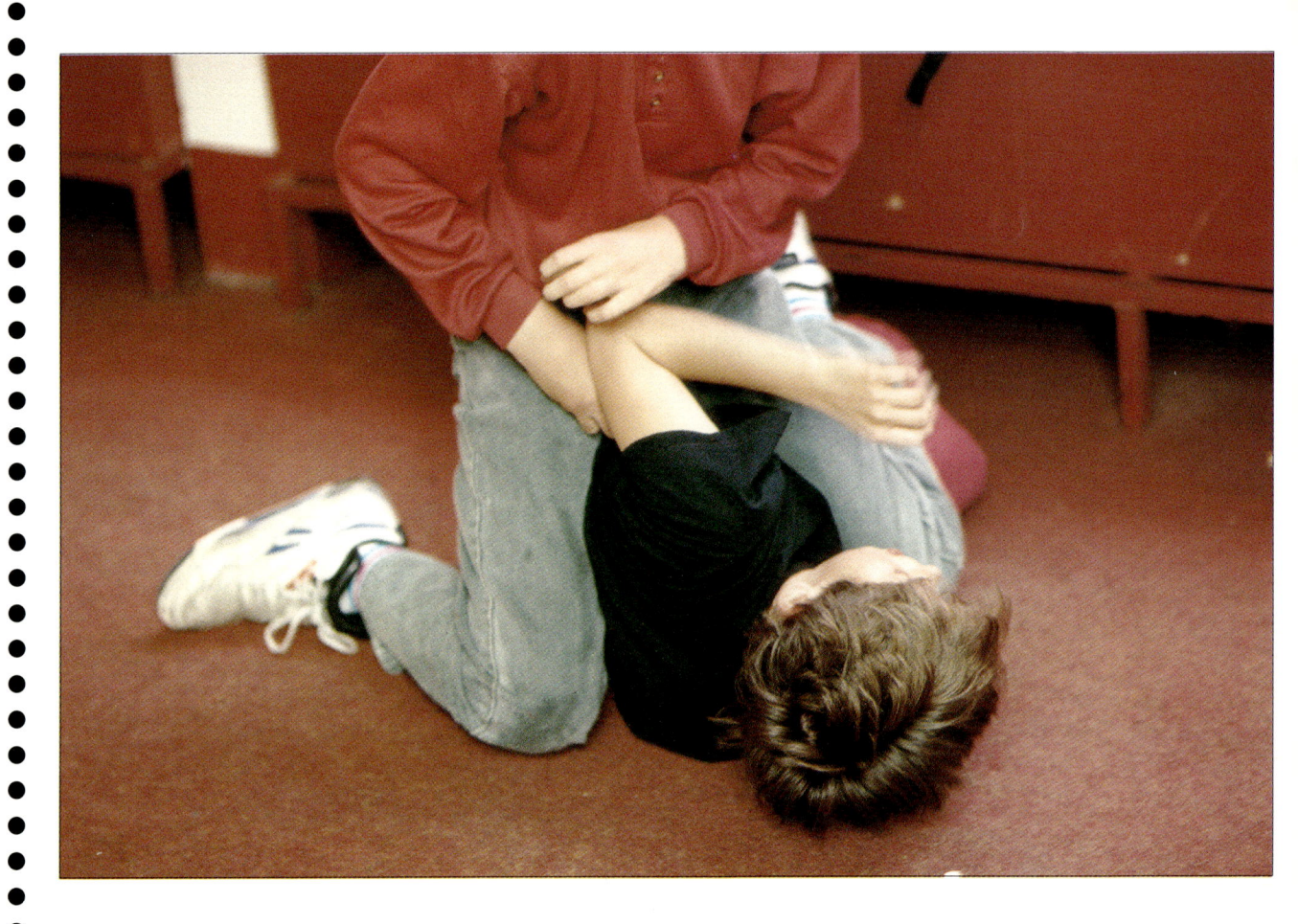

▲ If someone is bullied at home, by their parents or another adult, or by older brothers and sisters, they sometimes carry on that bullying outside home. They think that hurting others may make some of their own hurt go away.

Verbal bullying

As with physical bullying, the most effective way of dealing with verbal bullying is to stay calm. Don't react. Look confident. Again, you could try turning the whole thing into a joke. If you don't get upset or angry, the bully won't think you're worth picking on. If you know that you're likely to be bullied about something - your accent, perhaps - try replying in ways that make it look as though you don't care.

Or if you tend to get bullied because your parents are well-off, don't make the situation worse by wearing your best clothes and jewellery - it's not worth making an issue out of it.

A lot of verbal bullying involves doing things like spreading nasty rumours or singling someone out and refusing to talk to them. The only way to deal with this kind of behaviour is to make it plain that you're not bothered, even if you are. Bullies will soon get bored if you don't react.

Another bullying tactic is to tell everyone in the class something which is true but was supposed to be private between you and a friend. Again, if a bully threatens to spill the beans tell them you don't care if they do. Everyone does or says things they later wish they hadn't, and even the most embarrassing incidents are forgotten after a while. Try to remember something that embarrassed you in the past - it probably doesn't worry you so much now.

▼ **Don't be drawn into a bullying situation.** If people are talking about you behind your back, or are spreading rumours about you, just ignore them. Bullies want to make you miserable. If you don't appear upset, they will be wasting their time.

Group bullying/peer pressure

If you're being picked on by a whole gang, you might feel that there's not much you can do about it on your own. Keeping your confidence up when nobody seems to like you can be very hard.

Remember, though, how groups work: the chances are that quite a few people in the group wouldn't go along with the bullying if they had a choice, and certainly wouldn't do it if they were on their own. They probably find the pressure from others to join in is just too powerful to resist.

If that's the case, you might be able to confront them later with what they've done. Point out to these people that they're just as responsible as the group leaders for what's happened. Them saying 'It's not my fault, it was just what everyone was doing at the time' isn't good enough. Blame can't be made less by sharing it out.

You can use the same argument if you're part of a gang which is doing things you feel are wrong.

Others in the group might threaten you in order to make you join in, or you might be so worried about losing your friends that you feel forced to go along with it. If you don't like what is going on, there could well be others in the group who feel the same way.

Talk to them about it. Point out that you're all equally responsible and get them to help you stop the whole thing. If you can't get support, try to have the confidence to walk away.

▲ **Just because you're part of a group or gang doesn't mean you have to go along with everything the others do. Standing up for what you believe in can be tough, but you must do what you think is right.**

With all forms of bullying, there comes a point when you need to seek help from other people. The next chapter looks at different ways of doing this.

◄▼ Most of us like to be part of a group, and to have friends who we like and who like us. This can create a pressure to do 'anything' to remain part of the group.

HELPING YOURSELF 19

Getting adults involved

'*If you get it out in the open, you've got more chance of solving it* ' - secondary school student.

In one study of secondary school students, nearly three-quarters of those who reported being bullied had not told their teachers, and nearly two-thirds had not told their parents. When asked why, they said they were afraid that telling would get the bully into trouble, which would lead to further, and worse, attacks. They were worried about involving their parents or guardians because this might be embarrassing if they went to complain at school.

No one should have to suffer bullying and there is nothing wrong with asking for help. You are right to tell and you must keep on telling until you find someone who takes the whole issue seriously. Don't be put off by anyone who says you're being a wimp, or that the bullying will soon stop, or that you'll learn to cope with it.

▶ **Many victims simply don't tell because they blame themselves for what is going on - especially those who are bullied at home.**

BULLYING

▶ **Adults may be able to stop the bullying without it being obvious who's told them about it. If not, they can help to protect you from retaliation.**

Remember, bullying can only work if victims and their friends remain silent. It might help to get moral support from a friend or from someone who has seen you being bullied. But in order to stop the problem once and for all, you need to get adults involved.

Finding an adult you can trust and telling him or her can help in several different ways. For a start, if you're the victim of bullying you'll probably be feeling angry, frustrated, frightened and hurt. Your confidence might be at an all-time low and you may even blame yourself for what's happened and for not being able to stop it. A sympathetic adult can give support by just listening to you pour out your feelings.

It's important for adults to deal with bullies in a sensitive way. Bullies need handling firmly, but with care, if the problem is not to be made worse.

▲ Getting bullies to talk about how they feel and why they want to bully others is important if bullies and victims are to be together in the same school.

Anti-bullying policies in schools

One way of dealing with bullying at school is for teachers to treat it as a whole school issue, not just as a problem for particular individuals. By getting everyone involved and raising awareness of bullying, it's possible to create an environment where each person feels confident and good about him or herself.

▶ It helps to have a clear policy for dealing with bullying if it does happen. If your school doesn't have such an anti-bullying policy or charter, maybe you could suggest it to your class teacher or school council representative.

Such a policy might have three main goals:

1. To improve pupils' self-confidence.

2. To improve the school environment and make it a place where bullying is less likely to happen.

3. To improve everyone's awareness of bullying and its consequences.

Putting together a policy might include looking at who's likely to be bullied - new children and ethnic or cultural minorities, for example - and trying to improve their safety and confidence.

The next thing to do is to find out where bullying happens - the toilets, changing rooms, particular corridors, the playground, lesson changeover and sports lessons, for example. Increasing adult supervision at these times, or changing the timetable so that fewer children are in the corridors at any one time can help here.

If the school is very large, maps, signs and bright corridors will make it feel more friendly.

An anti-bullying charter draws everyone's attention to the problem of bullying, and the videos, plays and workshops listed at the end of this book make good starting points for discussion.

DEALING WITH

BULLYING

◀ **Unfortunately, most boarding shools have problems with bullying. Young people have to spend all their time together under one roof. This can lead to power battles, and to situations where bullies try to impress their 'weak' friends by picking on people.**

Bullying in institutions

Bullying at boarding schools can be particularly serious and frightening. There are plenty of opportunities for the bullies to go into action - at night and at weekends - and, because dormitories are shared, victims often have nowhere safe to retreat to. It's the same for people in residential care and young offender institutions, where newcomers are especially likely to be bullied.

If you're in any of these situations, talking to teachers or supervisors about bullying might be difficult without drawing attention to yourself.

If so, or if you cannot find a sympathetic adult to talk to, call or write to one of the organizations listed at the end of this book. Whatever you do, try and get help as soon as possible. If the bullies keep getting away with it, the bullying is likely to get worse and be harder to stop.

Help outside school and home

For some people, seeking help from teachers or parents will be difficult or impossible. Although an increasing number of teachers realise that bullying is a serious issue and want to stop it, not all will be sympathetic. Some may be bullies themselves. Others might hold the view that being bullied is an inevitable and even necessary part of fitting into school and learning to stand up for yourself.

Parents might also be unwilling to help for some reason. They may not have the confidence to contact your school, or they may think you're simply making a fuss and should cope on your own. Again, they may even be the ones doing the bullying.

If you can't get help from teachers or parents, contact Childline or one of the other organizations listed at the end of this book. If you can't use a telephone in private, write to them instead.

If you find you can't talk to an adult about the fact that you are being bullied, or, indeed, if you find that an adult can't or won't help, try talking to a friend. He or she is more likely to be on the same wavelength as you and better able to understand how you are feeling.

◀ Some schools pair up new children with older and more confident pupils who can introduce them to the school and keep an eye on them.

▼ If you are being bullied at school, it might help if you get moral support from a friend, or someone who has seen you being bullied.

What makes a bully?

Why some people bully

There are many different reasons why people get bullied. Children ringing into Childline's Bullying Line reported being bullied because they were fat, small for their age, had ginger hair or spots, were 'late' or 'early' developers, had shabby clothes, or had shoes or clothes that were too smart.

▶ **Bullies will always find some excuse to single out people to bully. They use reasons such as race, skin colour, religion, regional accent, social class, being bad at sports, having glasses or a brace, or simply being new. All these reasons mean that bullies have a huge number of people to pick on.**

But there are also many different reasons for someone becoming a bully and it helps to understand what some of them are.

When asked, some bullies have claimed that they were provoked by their victims. Others bullied simply because they didn't like the people they picked on, saying that they 'got on their nerves'.

BULLYING

WHAT MAKES A BULLY? 29

BULLYING

It seems that some people bully because they feel angry and upset about something, then get angry with others and take it out on them. Others just don't know any other way of behaving.

◀ **Some bullies come from homes where there's a lot of fighting instead of talking things through. They think it's OK to get their own way by being aggressive, because that's what they've learnt at home.**

An 'anxious bully' - someone who's not very confident and doesn't have many friends - gets a false feeling of confidence by intimidating and controlling other people. This kind is more likely to get involved in group bullying because being part of the group is more important to him or her than feeling bad about hurting others.

A 'bully/victim' - someone who has suffered from bullying themself - can turn to bullying as a way of asserting his or her own personality. It might be the only way they feel he or she can express themself. Or he or she might think that hurting others can somehow make his or her own hurt go away. It may also be the only kind of relationship that the bully knows.

▼ **Some people take part in group bullying because it gives then a false feeling of confidence. They don't think about the victim's feelings.**

WHAT MAKES A BULLY ?

How to help the bullies

Quite often bullies aren't the aggressive, confident individuals they make themselves out to be. A lot of them are actually rather anxious, insecure people. When bullies are asked how they feel, some do say that it makes them feel tough or hard, but others admit to feeling unhappy or bad about the way they behave. Perhaps this is because they know that what they're doing is wrong, but don't know how to stop themselves.

Of course bullies need to be handled firmly, but if they are to be helped they also need to be allowed to talk about what they do and why they do it. If they are victims of bullying themselves, then they must discuss their experiences and feelings. They also have to be encouraged to find other ways of feeling good about themselves.

Though they might think that bullying somehow makes them better, tougher or cleverer than others, they need to be shown that this is not so. And bullies who've somehow got away with this wrong behaviour in the past should be made aware that these kinds of tactics won't get them far when they become adults. Using violence as a way of dealing with problems is likely to land an adult bully in serious trouble.

Bullies should be made to think about other people's feelings, as well as their own. Everyone is different, so why pick on people because of the way they dress, or their accent, or the fact that they're overweight? Maybe the victims of bullying don't feel too happy about these aspects of themselves either. After all, nobody likes to stick out like a sore thumb.

▶ **Bullies like the feelings of power they get when they pick on people, especially if it is in front of an audience of people who are too weak or too scared to do anything but join in. In reality, bullies are often quite insecure people, lacking in self-confidence themselves.**

WHAT MAKES A BULLY ? 33

The importance of friends

◀▼ **Friends become especially important when you reach secondary school age. As you become more independent from your parents, and develop your own tastes, beliefs and interests, you'll want to spend more time with friends who share these ideas with you.**

As we've seen, both bullies and their victims are often people who lack self-confidence and find it hard to make friends. Usually the people who have few friends, who don't belong to a group and who don't have a high opinion of themselves end up being bullied. On the other hand, those doing the bullying are often people who feel that it's only by behaving in a hard or tough way that they can earn the admiration and friendship of others.

THE IMPORTANCE OF FRIENDS 35

Either way, friends play an important role in all our lives.

Everybody needs support from someone when things go wrong. When you were younger, you probably turned to your parents or guardian for help. They were the people who advised you about what did and didn't matter, and loved you no matter what.

Your parents or guardian can still do this for you, but the chances are that you won't always find your-selves on the same wavelength.

Parents or guardian won't always be able to see why something is so important to you, or why you want to go out with a particular person. They might be caught up in their own problems and unable or unwilling to listen to yours, or might find it hard to take them seriously. They simply might not be able to understand how you are feeling. This is where friends come in.

Because friends of the same age are going through the same kind of changes that all teenagers experience - changes in their bodies, changes in their emotions, and changes in their relationships with other people - they can be the people who really understand why things are important to you.

▲▶ **If you can learn to feel good about yourself, to concentrate on all your good points, and to accept that everyone is different, you may be on your way to finding it easier to make friends.**

THE IMPORTANCE OF FRIENDS

As well as listening to you, friends can come up with practical help in solving problems. If you're being bullied at school, friends can stick up for you and help keep your confidence up. If you need to talk to teachers or your parents about the bullying, friends can help by going with you as moral support.

Some people find it very hard to make friends and end up feeling lonely as a result. Shy people sometimes find it impossible to pluck up the courage to talk to someone new. Others might be different in some way, which for no good reason makes other people dislike them. For example, they may be overweight, or much less developed than others in their class, or they may have to wear braces on their teeth.

None of these things means that a person is not nice, or fun to be with. The problem is that they may not be given the chance to show that underneath they are the same as everyone else.

Sometimes lonely people put up a barrier between themselves and others so that they can't get hurt. They may pretend not to care about other people, or they may try to hurt others before they get hurt themselves. Unfortunately, this will only make them lonelier still.

If you find it hard to make friends, take a look at people who are popular. You'll probably notice that they're relaxed and confident, and don't seem worried about 'fitting in'. This doesn't mean that they don't have problems or that they don't wish they had smaller feet or thinner legs; they just don't let those things get them down.

Having made friends, some people seem to find it difficult to keep a friendship going. This could be for a variety of reasons. Perhaps they're the kind of person who demands too much from a friend. Or maybe they can't accept that their friend can also be close to someone else. Maybe they're unreliable and let people down. Or maybe they can't accept that someone can have different ideas and tastes from their own.

▶ **To keep a friendship going you need to be flexible without losing sight of the kind of person you want to be. It's important, too, to let others have their say - after all, they might be right! Most importantly, you need to be a good friend to others and to yourself.**

THE IMPORTANCE OF FRIENDS 39

Group work notes

Devising and conducting a bullying survey

One way to begin tackling the issue of bullying in your school or institution is to find out exactly what is happening by conducting a survey.

In groups, think through the issues around bullying and compile a questionnaire which can be completed in the playground. Information which you might hope to get could include: how many times people have been bullied recently, how many times they themselves have bullied, what people are bullied about, how people feel when they bully/are bullied/see bullying taking place, what sort of bullying is going on, what sort of people are bullies/are bullied, where and when bullying happens, what people do about it, and so on.

There's plenty to find out about, but don't make your questionnaire too long as it will be too difficult to analyse. Perhaps individual groups could tackle different questions. See if you can find any patterns in what people tell you: are there differences between what girls and boys say? How much racist and sexist bullying is there? Are there particular types of people involved? Are there particular times and places when bullying is likely to happen?

Feed back your information to the group, and perhaps use it for the next exercise.

Developing an anti-bullying policy

Read the section on anti-bullying policies in Chapter 3 and think about how you could develop an anti-bullying policy in your school or institution. In groups, discuss how you might go about tackling each of the three goals, and report back to the class.

Remember the goals are:
1. To improve everyone's self-confidence:

How can the safety and confidence of pupils who are likely candidates for bullying be improved?

How can everyone's self-esteem be raised? What about people who are not good at sports or academic subjects?

2. To improve the school/institution environment and make it a place where bullying is less likely to happen:

Where and when does bullying happen? How can it be reduced? Do the buildings, playgrounds or timetable encourage bullying? How can these be changed?

3. To improve everyone's awareness of bullying.

What can be done to make everyone in the school understand why bullying is an issue? How should an anti-bullying policy be publicized?

Lastly, plan out a display for the corridor of your school or institution based around a help and advice poster for people involved in bullying. Don't forget that your advice should be for witnesses and bullies as well as for victims.

The bully court

If bullying does happen, an effective way of dealing with it is to hold a bully court. As with a real court of law, anyone making a complaint of bullying against another pupil has to make a written statement in which they describe the events in question. The alleged bully must do the same.

A court hearing is arranged and the parents or guardians of the pupils concerned are told. The 'Bench' - a team of judges - is made up of pupils who are elected by other pupils, and possibly teachers.

The court procedure is to first ask the complainant (the victim) to give evidence, and then to answer questions put to him or her by the Bench. Then the defendant (the bully) is asked to give evidence and answer questions from both the Bench and the complainant. Witnesses can also be called and questioned. The members of the Bench discuss the evidence with some adults. They then give their conclusions and decisions on punishment, which the pupils themselves supervise.

Exercise

This exercise is not an *actual* bully court. It is to show how a bully court works and is a way of understanding it.

For this exercise, the group should form themselves into single-sex groups and plan a short role-play based on bullying situations which they are familiar with.

Everybody should have a role, even if it is as an onlooker. When each role play has been performed, the group should then choose one to use as the focus of the bully court. The remaining members of the group decide on the members of the Bench, and the bully court can proceed.

At the end of the court proceedings, group members can discuss their feelings about the issue, including their feelings in particular roles. They can also discuss what advice they would give to bullies, victims, teachers, parents and onlookers.

Helping agencies and organizations

1. Helplines

Anti-Bullying Campaign
Bristol
0272 264032

Cardiff
0222 758488

Cleveland
0642 584922

Croydon & Southeast
0737 242880

Halifax
0422 343282

Hertfordshire/London
081 906 3804

Lancashire/Yorkshire
05242 611125

Manchester
061 748 4338

Nottinghamshire
0602 636338

Sheffield
0742 455434

Worcester
0386 750872

Childline
0800 1111 (FREE)

Interlink
0504 271257

National Children's Home
Leeds
0532 456456

London
081 514 1177

Maidstone
0622 756677

Preston
0772 824006

NSPCC (National Society for the Prevention of Cruelty to Children)
0800 800500 (FREE)

RSSPCC (The Royal Scottish Society for the Prevention of Cruelty to Children)
031 337 8539

The Samaritans
0345 909090
(or look in your local phonebook, or ask the operator (dial 100) to put you through)

Wolverhampton Anti-Bullying Project
Helpline
0902 757513

2. Organizations

Advisory Centre for Education
(ACE) (Advice for parents)
1B Aberdeen Studios
22 Highbury Grove
London N5 2EA
071 354 8321

Anti-Bullying Campaign
(Support for parents of bullied children; resources for teachers)
18 Elmgate Gardens
Edgeware
Middlesex HA8 9RT
081 906 3804

and **44 Priory Drive**
Reigate
Surrey RH2 8AF
0737 242880

Campaign Against Bullying
(Campaigns and collects information on bullying in Ireland)
72 Lakelands Avenue
Upper Kilmacud Road
Stillorgan
Co. Dublin
Republic of Ireland
010 353 1 887976

Childline
(Helplines for children who are bullied or abused)
Second Floor
Royal Mail Building
Studd Street
London N1 0QJ
071 239 1000

Childline Midlands
Ashley House
331 Haydn Road
Sherwood
Nottingham NG5 1DG
0602 691199

Childline Scotland
33 Stockwell Street
Glasgow G11 4RZ
041 552 1123

Childline Wales
Royal Mail Building
15 Wind Street
Swansea SA1 1AA
0792 480111

If you want to write to Childline, you can do so without a stamp to:
Childline
Freepost 1111
London N1 0BR

Interlink
(Helpline and counselling for children who have been sexually abused and bullied)
12 Queen Street
Londonderry BT48 7EG
0504 266510

Kidscape
(Campaigns for children's personal safety and against bullying. Produces materials for schools)
152 Buckingham Palace Road
London SW1 9TR
071 730 3300

National Children's Home
(Support for families and young people, including those who have been bullied)
85 Highbury Park, London N5 1UD
071 226 2033

Wolverhampton Anti-Bullying Project (Helpline for children and parents, support for parents, and awareness of bullying issues in schools)
4 Crofters Walk
Dovecotes
Wolverhampton WV8 1UT
0902 757513

Resources: books, videos, playscripts, workshops

Books for young people

Bully by Yvonne Coppard (Bodley Head, 1990)
A new girl at school has a twisted leg and is called names and physically assaulted.

School Tales by Jill Dawson (Livewire, 1990)
Short stories written by young women, some involving bullying.

Annie on my Mind by Nancy Garden (Virago Upstarts, 1988)
Two seventeen-year-old girls are rejected by friends when it becomes known that they are having a close relationship.

Lord of the Flies by William Golding (Faber & Faber, 1954)
Classic story of boys on a desert island whose bullying of one boy ends in his death.

The Friends by Rosa Guy (Penguin, 1989)
An Afro-Caribbean girl is bullied at her new school, but finds an ally who stands by her against the bullies.

Speccy Four-eyes by Carole Lloyd (Julia MacRae, 1991)
A girl is bullied at school.

A Sense of Shame and Other Stories by Jan Needle (Armada, 1980)
Seven short stories about racial prejudice.

Don't Pick On Me by Rosemary Stones (Piccadilly, 1993)
A self-help book on how to handle bullying.

Roll of Thunder, Hear My Cry by Mildred D. Taylor (Penguin, 1988)
Semi-autobiographical novel set in the 1930s, about a black girl's experience of racial prejudice in Mississippi.

Playscripts

Only Playing, Miss!; Playscript Penny Casdagli and Francis Gobey with Caroline Griffin, Trentham Books, 1990
A play about bullying in secondary schools. Contains the playscript and accounts of reactions to the play.

The Bully
Glen Chandler, in Lifetime 1 ed Eurfrom Gwyne Jones, Cambridge University Press, 1982
The relationship between a bully and his victim is described.

Videos

Happy Memories
Tony Booth, Open University Course E242 Learning For All (Units 11-12) 1992
Television programme showing the reaction of one school to Neti-Neti's 'Only Playing, Miss!' (see below)
For information: Tony Booth, Open University, School of Education, Milton Keynes MK7 6AA, Tel: 0908 653770

Sticks and Stones
Central Independent Television, 1990
Video and information pack. Shows experiences of bullying, a bully court, children conducting a school survey and performing 'Only Playing Miss' (see below).

For information: Community Unit, Central Television, Broad Street, Birmingham B1 2JP.

My Life as Bully
Firehouse Productions
Humorous depiction of bullying in a comprehensive school.
For information: Firehouse Productions, 9 Clarendon Villas, Hove, East Sussex BN3 3RD.

Hands On Bullying
Tony Jewers Productions
Bullying in a secondary school and what to do about it.
For information:
Tony Jewers Productions, 4 Greystones Close, Colchester, Essex CO3 4RQ.

Only Playing, Miss!
Neti-Neti Theatre Company, 1990
Recording of Neti-Neti's play about bullying in school.
For information: Neti-Neti Theatre Company, 44 Gladsmuir Road, London N19 3JU.
Tel: 071 272 7302

Bullying in Schools
Delwyn Tattum and Graham Herbert, Drake Educational Associates, 1992
Videos and support materials from the authors of *Bullying - A Positive Response*
For information: Drake Educational Associates, St Fagan's Road, Fairwater, Cardiff CF5 3AE. Tel: 0222 560333

Workshops

Teenscape: A Personal Safety Programme for Teenagers
Michele Elliott, Health Education Authority, 1990
Workshop material for use by teachers, which covers a number of potentially dangerous situations and positive ways to deal with them, including bullying.

Only Playing, Miss!:
playscript/workshops
Penny Casdagli and Francis Gobey with Caroline Griffin, Trentham Books, 1990
Contains the playscript and a full description of the workshops.

Glossary

abuse Badly treating someone who is not in a position to defend his or herself. It can take the form of physical, sexual or mental maltreatment.

charter A document stating people's rights, usually drawn up after consultation with the people affected by the issues it concerns.

confidence Belief in yourself and your abilities. It is related to self-esteem, which is being able to like yourself without worrying what others think of you.

cultural/ethnic minority A group of people which is different from a larger group of which it is part, distinguished by race, religious beliefs, etc.

culture The music, learning, art, books, clothes, attitudes etc. of a society or group.

environment The place you are in, your surroundings or neighbourhood.

insecure. To feel insecure is to feel anxious and afraid, lacking in confidence.

moral suport Emotional help or encouragment given to a person in need.

peer Someone your own age from a similar social background.

peer pressure Imposing ideas on others of the same age and social background, or being encouraged or forced by others of your own age and background into doing something you don't want to do, such as smoking, taking drugs or bullying.

provocation Words or actions which are aimed at forcing you into some sort of reaction.

racism/sexism Something done in the belief that one race or one sex is better than another. Women suffer more from sexist behaviour by men, than men do by women.

retaliation An aggressive reaction to provocation.

Acknowledgements

Thanks to the following organizations which supplied the photographs used in this publication: Eye Ubiquitous 4, 6-7, 32-3; Sally and Richard Greenhill 5, 14, 16, 19 (top), 20; Robert Harding 10, 18; Reflections 8, 11, 15, 19 (bottom), 21, 22, 22-3, 24-5, 26-7, 31, 35, 36, 36-7, 38-9; Skjold 12; Tony Stone Worldwide 17 (Penny Tweedie), 28-9 (Lawrence Migdale), 34-5 (Penny Tweedie), 37 (Dale Durfee); Wayland Picture Library 30.

Index

anti-bullying policies 22-3, 46

boarding schools and bullying 25
bullies
  description of 8, 9, 12
  feelings of 28, 31, 32
  why bullies pick on particular people 11, 23, 28, 32
  why some people bully 28-31
bully courts 41
bully/victims 31
bullying
  effects of 4
  how it works 6, 12, 16, 21
bullying at home 9-10, 16
bullying surveys 40

calling names 6
Childline 9, 26, 28
confidence
  in bullies 12, 31, 32, 35
  in victims 11, 13, 14, 16, 17, 21, 23, 35, 38

feeling positive about yourself
  as part of stopping bullying 12

feelings
  about being bullied 5, 6, 10, 11, 26
  when bullying 9-10, 31
fighting 12-14
friends 34-8
  and bullying 8, 12-13
  support 26, 27, 38

group bullying 6, 12, 14, 31
  and peer pressure 8, 17-18

helping yourself 11-18, 36

joy-riding 8

loneliness 38

parents
  and bullying 9-10
peer group pressure
  and bullying 8, 17-18
physical bullying 6, 9, 10, 12-14

racial harassment 8-9
racist and sexist bullying 8-9
responsibility for behaviour
  when bullying 32

self-confidence 11, 12, 13, 14
self-defence 14
sexual abuse 10
sexual harassment 9
spreading rumours 16, 17
stopping bullying 14, 23, 36
support
  from friends and parents 26, 27

teachers
  and help with bullying 22, 25
teasing 5, 9
telling
  adults' attitudes to 21, 26
  teachers and parents 20, 22, 25
  threatening bullies with 14

verbal bullying 6, 10, 16
victims
  description of 4, 5, 10, 11

young offender institutions 25